UNDERGROUND
BRO
DECODER

HIDDEN MESSAGES
UNSOLVED **CASES**
SECRET DECODER **RING**

FINE print
PUBLISHING

UNDERGROUND
BRO
DECODER
CREATED BY
MICKEY
& CHERYL
GILL

TOP SECRET

Fine Print Publishing Company
P.O. Box 916401
Longwood, Florida 32791-6401

Created in the USA & Printed in China
This book is printed on acid-free paper.

ISBN 978-1-892951-89-2

2 4 6 8 10 9 7 5 3 1

fprint.net

AGENT

Sam

Last Name

EACH CASE,
FROM SINISTER PLOTS
TO LOST TREASURE,
STARTS WITH A

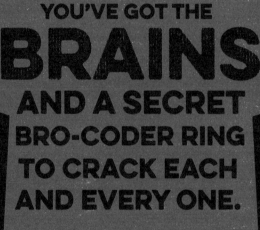

C⊙DE.

YOU'VE GOT THE

BRAINS

AND A SECRET
BRO-CODER RING
TO CRACK EACH
AND EVERY ONE.

PUT YOUR
SECRET AGENT

BRO-HOW

TO THE TEST!

HOW TO USE YOUR
SECRET
BRO-CODER RING

Look for the first letter of your message –
W – in the ring's inner circle first.

W is not there. So look for it in the outer circle.
Spin the ring's outer circle until you see the
letter **W** appear in the small window.

The letter that lines up directly below the
letter in the window is your first encoded letter.

Look for the second letter of your message – **A** – in the
ring's inner circle first. Now spin the ring's outer circle
until the window lines up directly above the letter.

The letter that appears in the window is
your second encoded letter.

Continue until you have completely encoded
your original message.

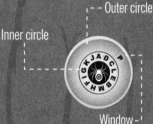
Inner circle
Outer circle
Window

W = J

A = N

Your coded message should read –

 JNGPU BHG SBE ZBAXRLF

FOLLOW THE
SAME STEPS
TO DECODE A
MESSAGE.

CODES VS. CIPHERS

CRACK THE CODE SOUNDS MORE AWESOME THAN **CRACK THE CIPHER!** SO, YOU'LL SEE THE WORD **CODE** MORE IN THIS BOOK. BUT REMEMBER, MOST **CODES** ARE REALLY **CIPHERS.** HERE'S THE DIFFERENCE.

CODES REPLACE AN ENTIRE WORD WITH A SET OF LETTERS, NUMBERS, OR SYMBOLS THAT ARE MADE UP.

SO THE WORD LEMON COULD BE #28.

CIPHERS REPLACE EACH LETTER IN A WORD WITH ANOTHER NUMBER, LETTER, OR SYMBOL.

SO THE WORD LEMON COULD BE YRZBA.

encode – convert into a coded form

encipher – convert a message or piece of text into cipher

decode – convert a code into language that can be understood

decipher – translate from secret or mysterious writing into normal language

encrypt – convert information or data into a cipher or code

decrypt – make a coded or unclear message understandable

YOU ARE AN OFFICIAL GOVERNMENT SPY.

YOU MUST ANSWER SOME TOP SECRET QUESTIONS SO HEADQUARTERS CAN ASSIGN YOU A FIELD AGENT POSITION.

GET GOING

Favorite kind of Saturday?

1. Doing as many different, awesome things as possible.

2. Sleeping in as long as I can

3. Doing something totally crazy with my friends.

How would your teacher describe you?

1. Gets along with teachers and lots of different kinds of kids.

2. Cool going solo or spending time with a few friends.

3. Friendly but a little mischievous.

There's a citywide volunteer cleanup day. You:

1. sign up on your own.

2. go because your parents make you

3. volunteer with a group of friends but goof off too much.

How daring are you?

1. Sort of but usually cautious.

2. Not. I'd rather relax.

3. Very! It's boring if you're not.

Best thing about a fair or theme park?

1. Hanging with friends

2. Food

3. Roller coasters!

Your teacher leaves the classroom for a few minutes. You:

1. talk to the kids around you in class.

2. kick back and chill at your desk.

3. throw paper balls at the back of your friends' heads.

Do you like learning other languages?

1. Yes, it's awesome.

2. It's OK.

3. Not really.

What kind of job sounds amazing?

1. Corporate president

2. Resort hotel employee

3. Outdoor sports & activities instructor

Who are you in your group of friends?

1. The leader

2. The cool one

3. The fun one

Would you like to live in another country?

1. I'm ready!

2. It might be OK.

3. Not feelin' it.

KEEP GOING

NEXT, ADD UP ALL THE NUMBERS YOU CIRCLED. IF YOUR TOTAL IS:

10-16, your code is – Q B H O Y R

17-23, your code is – F Y R R C R E

24-30, your code is – C E B I B X R E

WRITE YOUR CODE HERE.

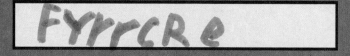

Fyrrcre

USE YOUR SECRET BRO-CODER RING TO DECIPHER YOUR CODE. ENTER IT BELOW.

LOOK FOR YOUR DECIPHERED WORD IN THIS LIST OF POSITIONS.

After you solve the cases inside, HQ will install you as a:

Double Agent/Operative

Infiltrate another country's intelligence agency. Work as if you are part of the agency. Gather important information and report back to HQ.

Sleeper Agent/Operative

Do nothing. Wait to be called on by HQ. Then follow instructions and complete your mission. Then wait again.

Provoker Agent/Operative

Go undercover, pretending to be part of an illegal organization. (It's being watched by HQ.) Get the organization to do something to get in trouble with local police.

How did you answer – Would you like to live in another country? If you answered . . .

1, Your post will be in another country.

2, You may go undercover in the US or abroad.

3, Your assignment will be stateside.

UNDERCOVER AGENT/ OPERATIVE PROCEDURES

You must complete these steps after agent orientation:

Create a **cover** as soon as possible.

COVER — identity, profession, activities used by an under-cover agent to hide his true identity and activities

LEGEND — spy's claimed back-ground or life story, supported by documents and memorized details

Back up your cover with a detailed **legend**.

HANDLER — case officer who is responsible for directing agents in operations

Arrange a meeting with your **handler**.

PROJECT MI AGENT
CASE NO. TOP SECRET

TOP SECRET

FOR YOUR EYES ONLY

YOUR SECRET AGENT
PARTNER,
TY DUP,
HAS BEEN
CAPTURED.

HE WILL FIND
YOU WHEN HE
ESCAPES.

BACKGROUND:

Before your partner was taken by enemy operatives, he left you a coded message.

BRO-CODER RING

PBIRE OYBJA.
1. PUNATR ANZR.
2. TRG QVFTHVFR.
3. ZBIR.

DECIPHER THE MESSAGE BELOW.

_____ .

1. _____ .

2. _____ .

3. _____ .

1. YOU CANNOT USE YOUR SECRET AGENT NAME ANYMORE.

ASSIGN YOURSELF A NEW NAME. LOOK FOR THE SECOND LETTER IN YOUR FIRST NAME (BOLD BLACK TYPE) IN THIS LIST.

AMOS	**H**ORACE	**O**SWALD	**V**IRGIL
BERTRAM	**I**GOR	**P**HINEAS	**W**ILBUR
CALVERT	**J**ASPER	**Q**UENTIN	**X**AVIER
DUDLEY	**K**ILGOR	**R**EGINALD	**Y**UL
ELMER	**L**OWELL	**S**HERMAN	**Z**ED
FELIX	**M**ORTIMER	**T**HURLOW	
GROVER	**N**EVILLE	**U**LYSSES	

NOW LOOK FOR THE SECOND LETTER OF YOUR LAST NAME IN THIS LIST.

ARMPIT	**H**AIRYBACK	**O**TTERBREATH	**V**ACUUMLINT
BUTT	**I**CK	**P**ICKLEFEET	**W**ORMFEST
CRUMP	**J**UICEBOX	**Q**UACKMASTER	**X**YLOPHONE
DUNGBEETLE	**K**ICKBUTT	**R**UNNYNOSE	**Y**AKEATER
EGGHEAD	**L**ONGBOTTOM	**S**WEATPANTS	**Z**OOKEEPER
FISHLIPS	**M**ONKEYBREATH	**T**WOTONGUES	
GATORBUMPS	**N**OSEHAIR	**U**NDERPANTS	

ENTER YOUR NEW FIRST & LAST NAME BELOW.

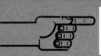

PROJECT MI AGENT
CASE NO 135

2. CHANGE YOUR HAIR OR FACE.

COUNT THE NUMBER OF LETTERS IN YOUR ORIGINAL FIRST, MIDDLE, AND LAST NAME.

IF THE NUMBER OF LETTERS IS . . .

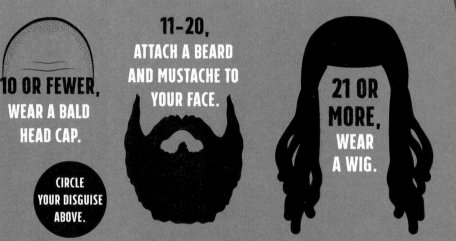

10 OR FEWER, WEAR A BALD HEAD CAP.

11-20, ATTACH A BEARD AND MUSTACHE TO YOUR FACE.

21 OR MORE, WEAR A WIG.

CIRCLE YOUR DISGUISE ABOVE.

3. CIRCLE SOME PROPS TO COMPLETE YOUR DISGUISE.

MOTORCYCLE

TUXEDO

BOOTS

GOLF CLUBS

SURFBOARD

BACKPACK

BASEBALL CAP

FAKE TATTOOS

SPORTS CAR

LEATHER JACKET

FLIP-FLOPS

GUITAR

4. RELOCATE TO A NEW AREA.
USE THE MONTH YOU WERE BORN TO IDENTIFY THE AREA YOU WILL MOVE TO.

JAN – JACKSON, WYOMING

FEB – FIJI

MAR – MANITOBA

APR – ANTARCTICA

MAY – MAUI, HAWAII

JUN – JUNEAU, ALASKA

JUL – JODHPUR, INDIA

AUG – AUSTRIA

SEP – SAHARA DESERT

OCT – OSLO, NORWAY

NOV – NETHERLANDS

DEC – DECATUR, GEORGIA

ENTER YOUR NEW LOCATION BELOW.

PROJECT MI AGENT

CASE NO 135

DOT CIPHER

PUT YOUR AGENT BRO-HOW KNOWLEDGE TO THE TEST

1. Carefully cut out this alphabet strip along the dotted line.

A B C D E F G H I J K L M N O P Q R S T U V W X Y Z

2. Place the alphabet strip on the first line of the notebook paper below. Line up the left side of the strip with the notebook paper margin (red line).

3. Write the letter that appears directly above dot.

4. Move alphabet strip down to next line. Keep left side of the strip lined up with notebook paper margin! Write the letter that appears directly above dot.

5. Continue moving down notebook paper and writing letters. They will reveal a top secret message from HQ.

PROJECT PORTAL PRINCE
CASE NO. 1353

CONFIDENTIAL

BACKGROUND:

The family that lives in the castle has never known where to find the portal.

Recently, a stranger showed up and started asking the family a lot of really nosy questions about the castle.

Suspicious visitor

MATERIALS:

An unusual note has been passed down through the family for hundreds of years. No one understands it. It doesn't make sense. The note might be a clue.

PROJECT PORTAL PRINCE
CASE NO. 1353

Study and decipher the note's meaning to see if it's a clue. Locate the portal before it's too late.

E T R N T E W R D E I D S I O A M R

N E A O H R O L B H N A U T F R O

Look for a pattern in the note.

Connect letters, moving up and down, right to left, horizontally, etc. like this.

E T R   E→T R E T R
OR   OR
N→E A   N→E A   N E A

See if words start to form. When words start to form, continue connecting letters in that same pattern. Write the string of letters below. Look for the message.

UNDERCOVER AGENT/ OPERATIVE PROCEDURES

You must complete these steps before reporting to your post:

COBBLER — (a.k.a. shoemaker) spy who creates/forges false passports, visas, diplomas and other documents

SHOE — false passport or visa

Visit a **cobbler** immediately so he can work on your **shoe**.

POCKET LITTER — items in an agent's pocket — receipts, tickets, scribbled-on scraps of paper, etc. that make his identity believable

Create some **pocket litter**. Stash it in your pockets, backpack, and bags.

PAROLES — passwords agents use to identify themselves to each other

Memorize your **paroles** and use when dealing with other agents.

PROJECT KNOCK OC
CASE NO. 8

CONFIDENTIAL

FOR YOUR EYES ONLY

LEGEND HAS IT THA
TREASURE OFF THE
REMOTE ISLAND. A
CREW, HOPING TO FI ID
IS LOOKI.JG FO

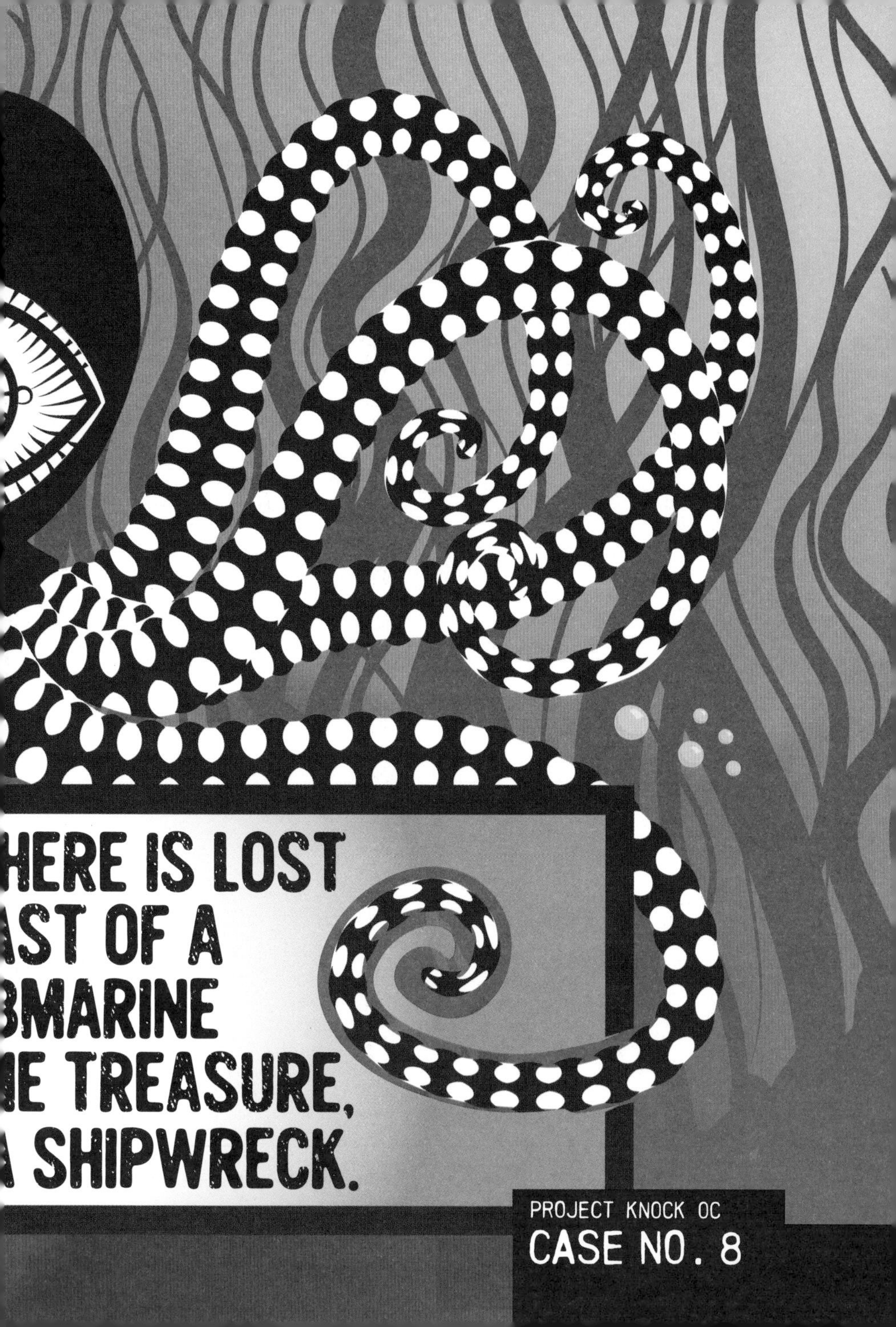

HERE IS LOST
AST OF A
BMARINE
IE TREASURE,
A SHIPWRECK.
PROJECT KNOCK OC
CASE NO. 8

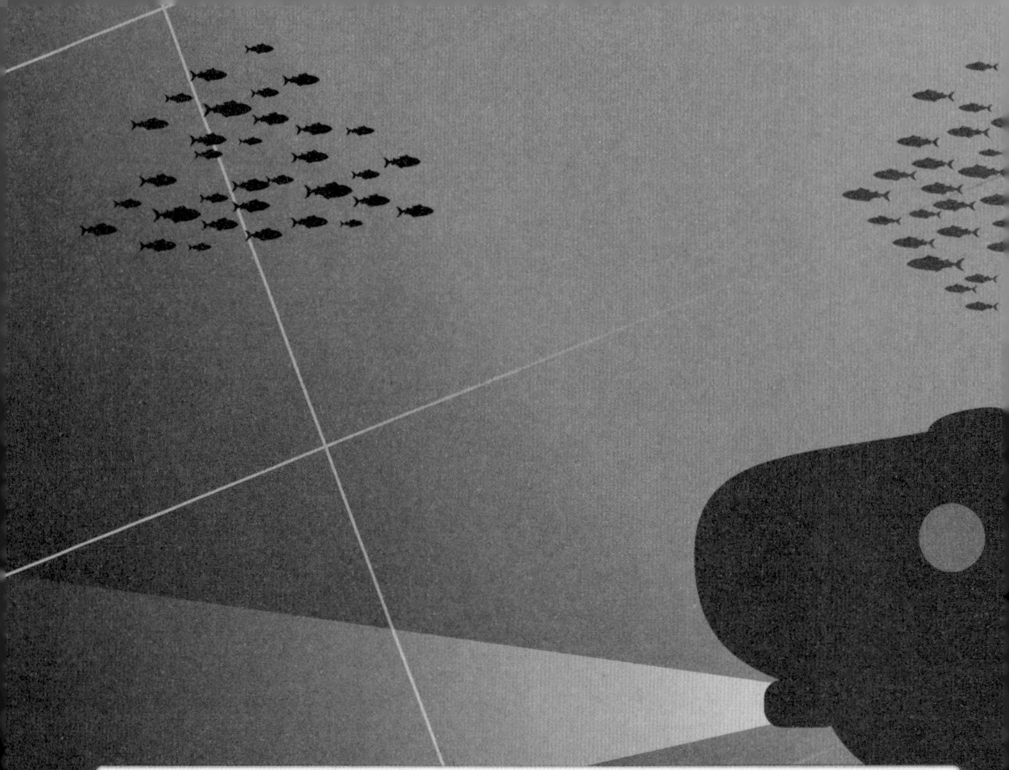

BACKGROUND:

THE SUBMARINE CREW IS ABOUT TO GIVE UP ITS SEARCH. THE CREW CANNOT LOCATE A SHIP-WRECK, AND AN OCTOPUS IS INTERFERING WITH THE MISSION. THE OCTOPUS IS KNOCKING AGAINST THE SUB EVERY DAY.

PROJECT KNOCK OC
CASE NO. 8

DETAILS:

THERE IS A PATTERN TO THE OCTOPUS KNOCKS. IT'S A SET OF SHORT AND LONG KNOCKS.

ASSIGNMENT:

USE MORSE CODE TO TRY TO DECODE THE OCTOPUS KNOCKS AND HELP THE CREW.

MORSE CODE

A •-				
B -•••	G --•	L •-••	Q --•-	V •••-
C -•-•	H ••••	M --	R •-•	W •--
D -••	I ••	N -•	S •••	X -••-
E •	J •---	O ---	T -	Y -•--
F ••-•	K -•-	P •--•	U ••-	Z --••

CREW'S LOG OF OCTOPUS KNOCKS

DASHES ARE LONG KNOCKS

DOTS ARE SHORT KNOCKS

DECODE CREW'S LOG BELOW

THE CREW HAS BEEN LOOKING FOR A SHIP.
WHAT SHOULD THEY REALLY BE LOOKING FOR?

PROJECT KNOCK OC
CASE NO. 8

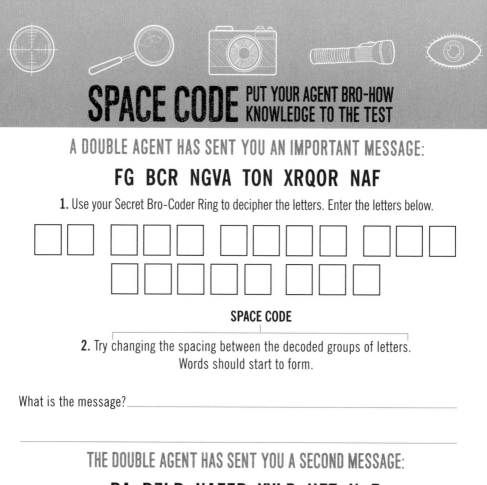

SPACE CODE PUT YOUR AGENT BRO-HOW KNOWLEDGE TO THE TEST

A DOUBLE AGENT HAS SENT YOU AN IMPORTANT MESSAGE:

FG BCR NGVA TON XRQOR NAF

1. Use your Secret Bro-Coder Ring to decipher the letters. Enter the letters below.

SPACE CODE

2. Try changing the spacing between the decoded groups of letters. Words should start to form.

What is the message? _____

THE DOUBLE AGENT HAS SENT YOU A SECOND MESSAGE:

RA RZLP NAFZR YYLB HET N F

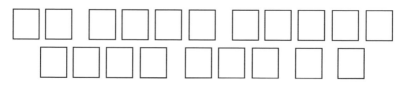

Use your Secret Bro-Coder Ring and Space Code to decipher it.

What is the message? _____

PROJECT SUPER SAVE
CASE NO. 86

CONFIDENTIAL

FOR YOUR EYES ONLY

THE WORLD'S SUPERHEROES ARE IN GRAVE DANGER!

UNIVERSE SECURITY EMERGENCY

DR. BO OGER

AN EVIL SCIENTIST, DR. BO OGER, HAS CREATED A VIRUS THAT STRIPS SUPERHEROES OF ALL METAHUMAN POWERS. HE'S STORING IT IN HIS COMPOUND'S SECRET VAULT.

PROJECT SUPER SAVE
CASE NO. 86

ASSIGNMENT:

YOU AND A TEAM OF NINJAS MUST SNEAK ONTO DR.OGER'S COMPOUND, ENTER THE CODE TO HIS VAULT, STEAL THE VIRUS, & SAVE THE DAY.

DR. BO OGER'S COMPOUND

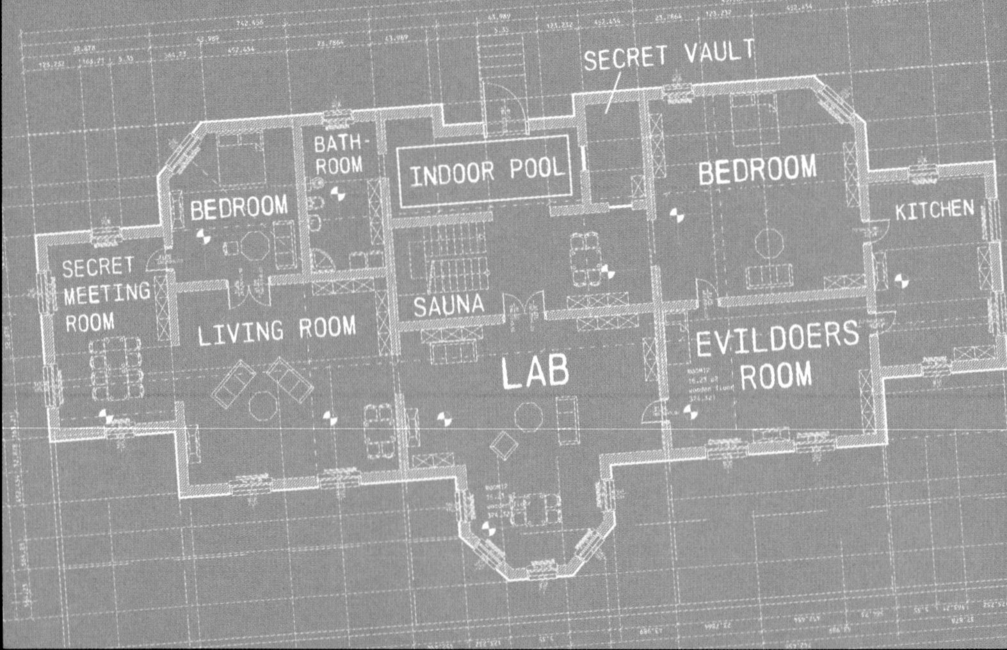

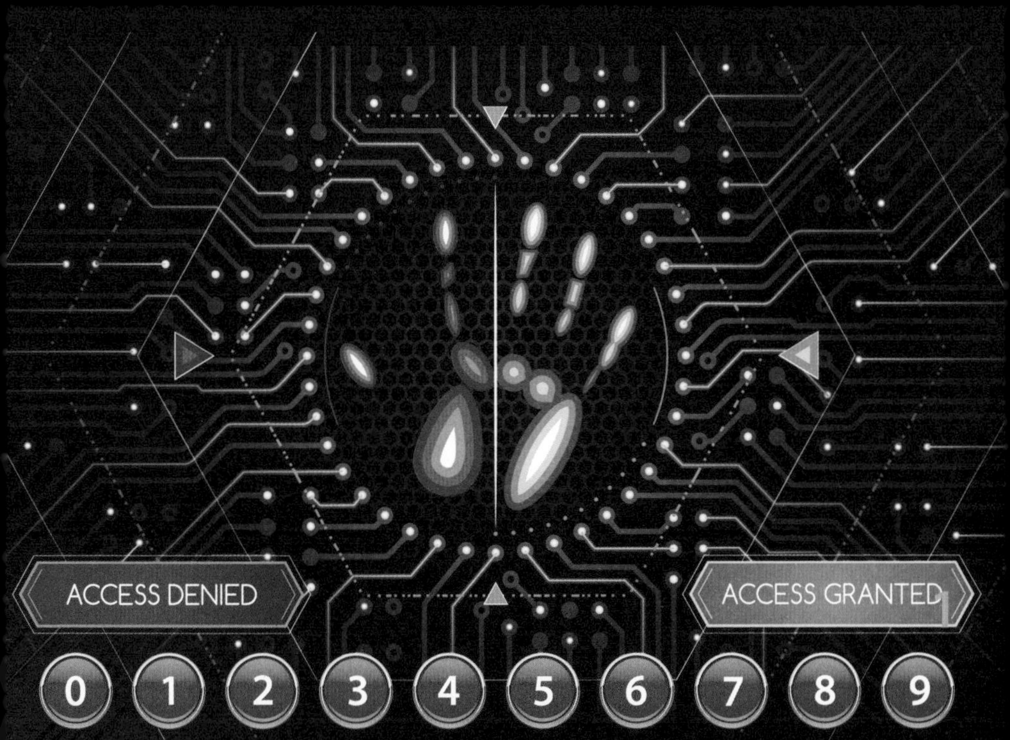

EVIDENCE:

HEADQUARTERS INTERCEPTED THREE NOTES FROM THE DOCTOR'S MINIONS. THEY MIGHT INCLUDE A VAULT NUMBER CODE. DECIPHER THE NOTES AND FIND OUT.

PROJECT SUPER SAVE

CASE NO. 86

USE THE GRID BELOW TO DECIPHER
THE NOTES TO THE RIGHT. EACH
LETTER = A PAIR OF NUMBERS.
U=45 (**U** IS IN ROW 4, COLUMN 5).
P=35 (**P** IS IN ROW 3, COLUMN 5).
SO THE WORD **UP**=45 35.

THESE ②LETTERS SHARE THE SAME NUMBER.
SEE WHICH LETTER MAKES THE MOST SENSE IN A WORD.

COLUMNS

	1	**2**	**3**	**4**	**5**
1	A	B	C	D	E
2	F	G	H	I/J	K
3	L	M	N	O	P
4	Q	R	S	T	U
5	V	W	X	Y	Z

ROWS

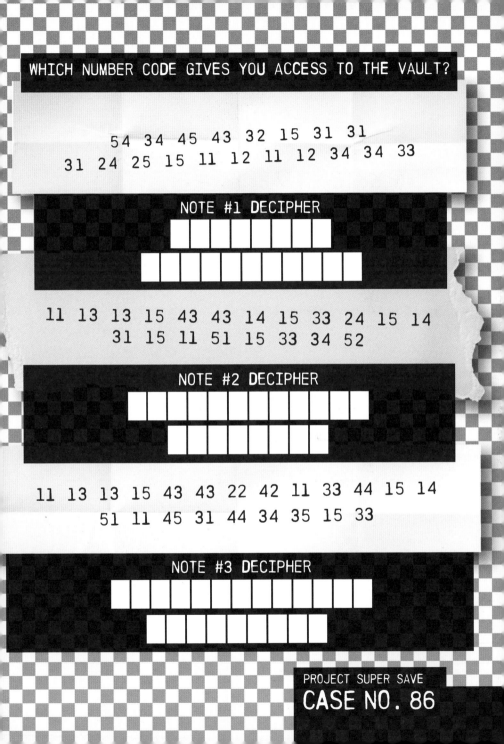

UNDERCOVER AGENT/ OPERATIVE MANEUVERS

Follow these directives for passing information:

BRIEF ENCOUNTER — any brief physical contact between a case officer and an agent under threat of surveillance

Plan **brief encounters** in crowded, public areas to interfere with any possible surveillance.

BRUSH PASS — brief encounter when an item is passed between case officer and agent — appear to "brush" by or bump into each other

Complete a **brush pass** only if you believe it will go completely undetected.

LIVE LETTER DROP — agent follows a path on foot with document hidden in a pocket. Second agent, unknown to the first, "picks" his pocket and passes document to a **cut-out** or officer

Plan any **live letter drops** well in advance.

CUT-OUT — person or mechanism used by agents to pass material or message safely

PROJECT MOLE IN THE HOLE
CASE NO. 1111

CONFIDENTIAL

BACKGROUND:

A RING OF INTERNATIONAL SPIES IS MEETING IN A MAJOR CITY'S NETWORK OF UNDERGROUND TUNNELS. THE RING WORKS FOR AN ORGANIZATION THAT'S PLOTTING WORLD DOMINATION.

PROJECT MOLE IN THE HOLE
CASE NO. 1111

ASSIGNMENT:

GO UNDERCOVER AND INFILTRATE THE RING. YOU ARE THE MOLE.

YOUR JOB IS TO REPORT THE PLANS TO HEADQUARTERS.

[infiltrate – move into an organization secretly and cause the downfall of.]

MATERIALS:

[intercept – take, seize, or halt.]

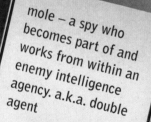

mole – a spy who becomes part of and works from within an enemy intelligence agency. a.k.a. double agent

HQ INTERCEPTED A CODED TEXT MESSAGE FROM ONE OF THE SPIES.

IT MAY CONTAIN THE LOCATION AND TIME OF NEXT UNDERGROUND MEETING. HQ THINKS THE SPIES USED A KEYBOARD CIPHER.

HOW THE KEYBOARD CIPHER WORKS

To code a message, find the letter you need to code on a keyboard. Then move either 1, 2, 3, or 4 keys **to the left**. This is your coded letter.

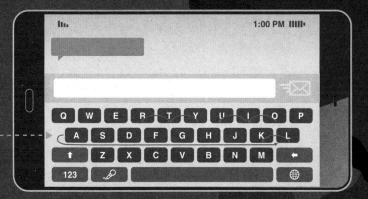

Try coding the message
YOU ARE THE MOLE

Base your code on moving 2 keys **to the left**.
Y=R, O=U, and U=T.

When you use a letter on the far left of the keyboard, like A, wrap around to the end of that letter's row for your first move.
Then move to the left. So A = K.
(Skip any punctuation or command keys on a computer keyboard. Do not count.)

YOU ARE THE MOLE=
RUT KWQ EFQ BUJQ

Find the first letter of the coded text message (W) on the keyboard. Move either 1, 2, 3, or 4 keys **to the right**.

When you use a letter on the far right of the keyboard, like P, wrap around to the beginning of that letter's row for your first move.

Try this with the first coded word until a real word forms. Then continue to use that same pattern of key moves to decode the rest of the message. Write message below.

Mark the location of the next spy ring meeting.

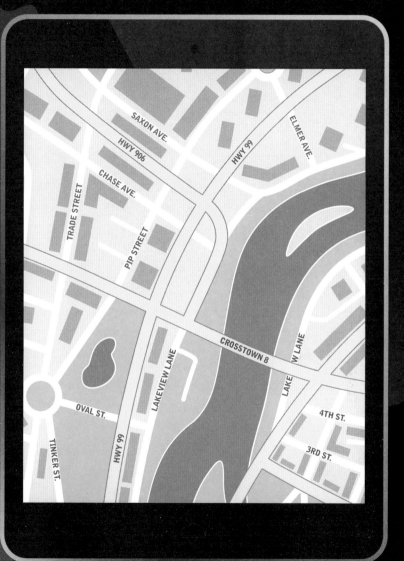

The note below contains a message within another message. The first letter of each word forms the original message (or, **plain text**) when strung together.

> **plain text** – original readable text; not a coded version.

Circle the first letter of each word within this strange message.

Clever orangutans verified electronic rainbows in snowy blue landslides on Wednesday night.

What is the message? _____

HQ HAS SENT YOU AN IMPORTANT ENCRYPTED MESSAGE:

Hey cool Ukulele Mary, keep playing during rowing season. Taxing shiny cases stopped tourist site from offering lockets. Slow, sandy otters carry broccoli lollipops.

Try circling the first, second, or third letter of each word until you see words start to form. Once you do, continue using that same pattern. Write the letters down.

Write the string of letters below.

_____

What is the message?

_____

PROJECT INSECTICYBORG
CASE NO. OO6

CONFIDENTIAL

A NOTORIOUS BAND OF EVIL
ELITE FORCE
SUPER CYB

ERS HAVE ENGINEERED AN
F DANGEROUS,
ORG BUGS.

THE GROUP CROSSED THE
DNA OF FIVE DIFFERENT
INSECTS AND ADDED
ROBOTICS. THEIR INSECT
ARMY MUST BE STOPPED.

STATUS:

YOUR SECRET AGENT PARTNER HAS DISCOVERED THE EVIL GROUP'S SCIENTIFIC PLANS. HE HAS SENT YOU A CODED MESSAGE. IT IS A LIST OF THE FIVE INSECTS USED TO CREATE THE SUPER BUGS.

ASSIGNMENT:

USE YOUR SECRET BRO-CODER RING TO DECODE YOUR PARTNER'S MESSAGE. GIVE THE LIST TO HQ'S LAB. THE LAB WILL USE IT TO MAKE A SUPER INSECTICIDE.

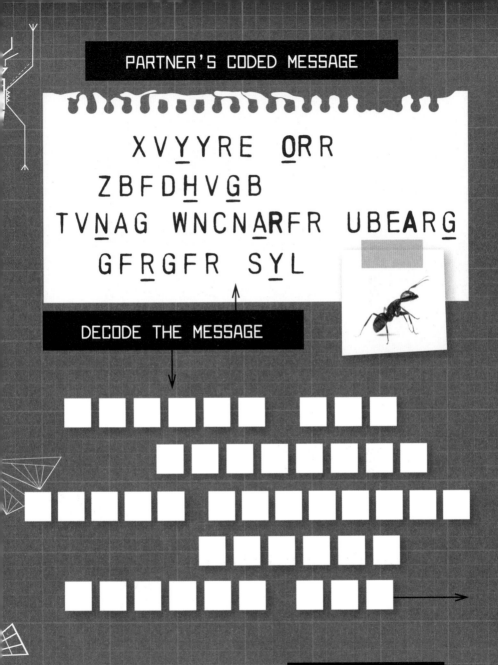

XVYYRE ORR
ZBFDHVGB
TVNAG WNCNARFR UBEARG
GFRGFR SYL

DECODE THE MESSAGE

PROJECT INSECTICYBORG
CASE NO.006

YOU STILL NEED THE NAME OF
THE FIFTH INSECT. YOUR PARTNER
MAY HAVE HIDDEN THE NAME IN
HIS CODED MESSAGE OR
LEFT YOU A CLUE.

YOUR PARTNER'S CODED MESSAGE
INCLUDES SOME UNDERLINED LETTERS.
ENTER THEM BELOW.

DECODE THE LETTERS USING YOUR BRO-CODER RING.

WHAT KIND OF INSECT IS ON THE PAPER
TAPED TO YOUR PARTNER'S CODED MESSAGE?
ENTER THE NAME OF IT HERE.

NOW CROSS OUT THE NAME OF THE INSECT
IN THE DECODED SET OF LETTERS ABOVE.

UNSCRAMBLE THE LEFTOVER LETTERS
UNTIL THEY FORM A WORD.
ENTER THEM HERE.

5TH INSECT

PROJECT INSECTICYBORG
CASE NO.006

DOCUMENTS & INFORMATION CLASSIFICATIONS

You may be granted clearance to read materials or hear information with these different designations:

CLASSIFIED — designated as officially secret; only authorized people may have access to

Classified information is marked **CONFIDENTIAL**, **SECRET** and **TOP SECRET**

CONFIDENTIAL
unauthorized release could cause damage to national security

SECRET
security classification above confidential and below top secret

more restrictions than confidential

unauthorized release could cause serious damage to national security

TOP SECRET
of the highest secrecy; highly confidential

highest security classification; unauthorized release could cause exceptional damage to national security

more restrictions than secret

PROJECT GREEN MACHINE
CASE NO. 21

CONFIDENTIAL

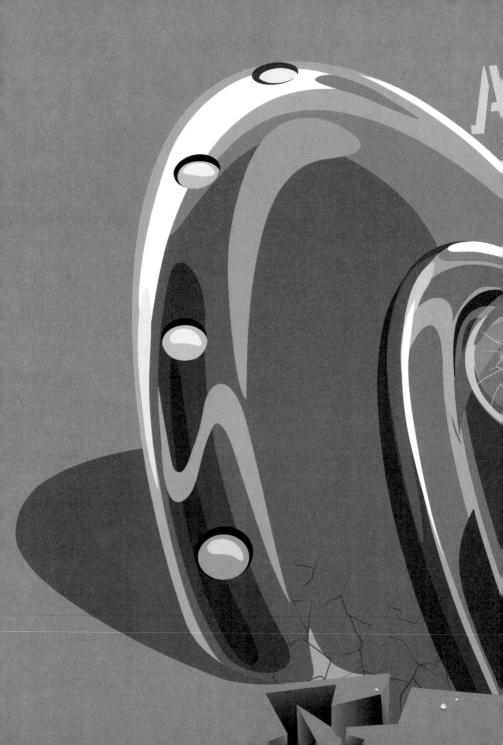

UFO crash site has been discovered.

A strange message is carved into the side of the ship.

PROJECT GREEN MACHINE
CASE NO. 21

Some of the symbols in the message are worn off.
RADIOACTIVE HAZARD

MATERIALS:

Investigators believe this ancient tablet is the key to deciphering it.

ASSIGNMENT:

Decipher the coded symbols. Then guess what letters are missing. Fill in the missing letters & matching symbols.

The missing symbols in the extraterrestrial code may not be an accident.

Fill in the four missing symbols below, in the order they appear in the message.

Turn this book until you see a message appear. Write the one-word message below.

During the investigation, an alien made contact with an agent and handed him this document. It may help you.

A	Beware of
B	Headed your way
C	Take us to your leader
D	We're preparing to
E	Coming to
F	Put up force shields
G	Do not land on
H	Enemy aliens
I	Saturnians
J	Eat people
K	Assist you
L	Capture us
M	Will exterminate aliens

N	Do not engage with
O	Join forces with
P	Take over Earth
Q	Intergalactic allies
R	Travelling to
S	Fleet of ships is
T	Universe in peril
U	Destruction is imminent
V	Jupiter
W	Prepare for battle
X	Arm yourself with ray guns
Y	Another universe
Z	Martians

Use the document to decipher the one-word message. Write it below.

ROUTE CIPHER
PUT YOUR AGENT BRO-HOW KNOWLEDGE TO THE TEST

HQ HAS SENT YOU AN IMPORTANT ENCRYPTED MESSAGE:
SIY OSO MSU ETR TUT HCE IKE NIT GNH

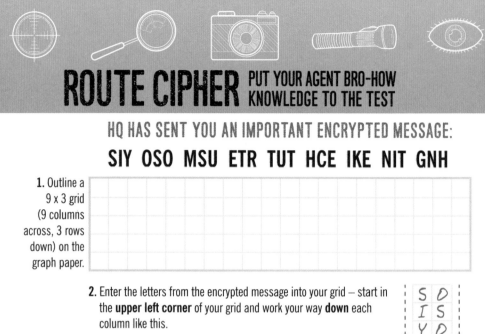

1. Outline a 9 x 3 grid (9 columns across, 3 rows down) on the graph paper.

2. Enter the letters from the encrypted message into your grid — start in the **upper left corner** of your grid and work your way **down** each column like this.

3. Now reading across each row from left to right, write the string of letters below. What is the message?

HQ HAS SENT YOU A SECOND ENCRYPTED MESSAGE:
NRNII EGABT EDGSI

1. Outline a 3 x 5 grid (3 columns across, 5 rows down) on the graph paper.

2. Enter the letters from the encrypted message into your grid — start in the **bottom right corner** and work your way **up** each column.

3. Now reading across each row from left to right, write the string of letters below. What is the message?

PROJECT MYSTERY MAIL
CASE NO. 48

POST OFFICE
★ 04.08.2055 ★
POST OFFICE

CONFIDENTIAL

FOR YOUR EYES ONLY

TOP SECRET DOCUMENTS HAVE BEEN SHOWING UP AT YOUR HOUSE.

PROJECT MYSTERY MAIL
CASE NO. 48

BACKGROUND:

YOU HAVE RECEIVED FOUR CODED DOCUMENTS OVER THE PAST YEAR. THERE'S NO SIGNATURE OR RETURN ADDRESS. THEY'RE NOT FROM HEADQUARTERS.

LAB RESULTS:

HQ'S TESTS ONLY SHOW YOUR DNA ON THE DOCUMENTS. THE LAB HAS ASKED YOU TO WEAR GLOVES TO OPEN MAIL FROM NOW ON.

ASSIGNMENT:

STUDY THE DOCUMENTS AND FIGURE OUT THE COMMUNI-CATION. THE FOURTH ONE MAY BE A CODE KEY.

ABC	DEF	GHI
JKL	MNO	PQR
STU	VWX	YZ

THIS MAY BE A CODE KEY FOR THE REST OF THE DOCUMENTS.

LINES ARE USED TO SHOW THE PART OF THE GRID THE LETTER IS IN. A DOT SHOWS WHERE THE LETTER IS LOCATED WITHIN THE GROUP OF THREE LETTERS. SO,

A = .⌐   B = .⌐   AND C = _.⌐

M = ⌐.   AND Q = ⌐.

USE THE CODE KEY TO DECIPHER EACH DOCUMENT.

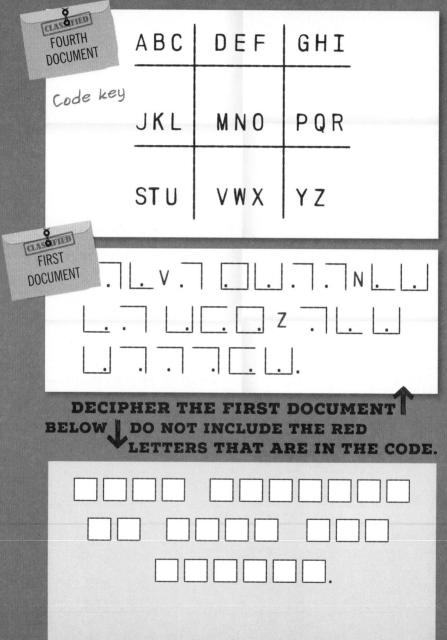

CLASSIFIED
FOURTH
DOCUMENT

Code key

ABC	DEF	GHI
JKL	MNO	PQR
STU	VWX	YZ

CLASSIFIED
FIRST
DOCUMENT

DECIPHER THE FIRST DOCUMENT BELOW DO NOT INCLUDE THE RED LETTERS THAT ARE IN THE CODE.

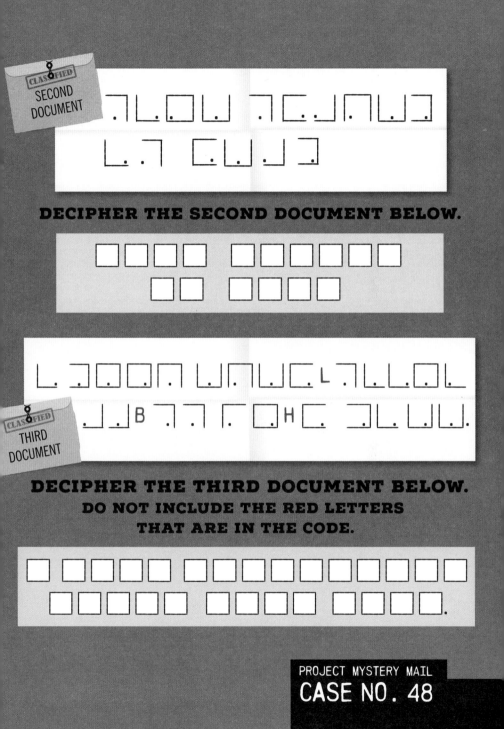

DECIPHER THE SECOND DOCUMENT BELOW.

DECIPHER THE THIRD DOCUMENT BELOW.
DO NOT INCLUDE THE RED LETTERS
THAT ARE IN THE CODE.

PROJECT MYSTERY MAIL
CASE NO. 48

1. USE YOUR SECRET BRO-CODER RING TO DECIPHER THE SIX RED LETTERS (V, N, Z, L, B, AND H) THAT ARE IN THE ORIGINAL CODED DOCUMENTS. ADD THEM TO YOUR DECIPHERED DOCUMENT MESSAGES TO COMPLETE WORDS.

2. NOW WRITE THESE SAME SIX DECIPHERED LETTERS BELOW, IN THE EXACT ORDER THEY APPEARED IN THE DOCUMENTS.

☐ ☐ ☐ ☐ ☐ ☐

WHO IS THE MYSTERY MAN SENDING THESE DOCUMENTS?

PROJECT MYSTERY MAIL
CASE NO. 48

CREATE YOUR OWN
CODE OR CIPHER
BELOW. USE WITH SECRET AGENTS,
BROS, & OTHER LIFE FORMS.

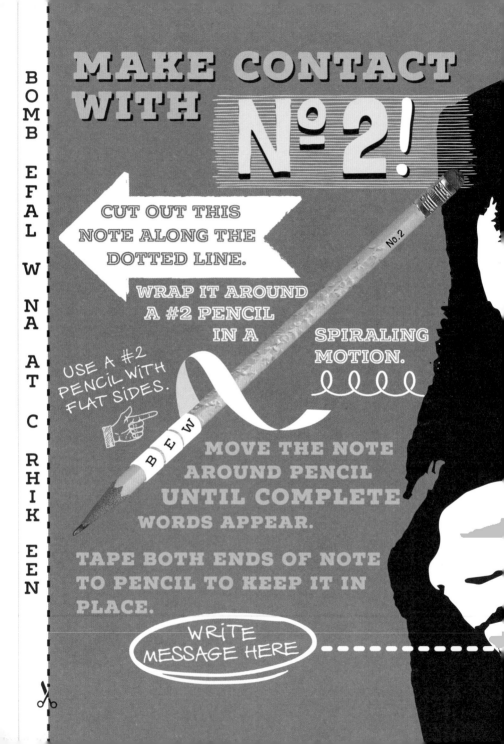

TURN HERE
FOR MORE
#2

CUT OUT THESE BLANK NOTES
ALONG THE DOTTED LINES.

WRAP A NOTE AROUND A #2
PENCIL IN A SPIRALING MOTION.

TAPE BOTH ENDS OF
THE NOTE TO PENCIL TO KEEP
IT IN PLACE.

WRITE MESSAGE TO A **BRO** ON
THE FLAT SIDES OF A PENCIL
LIKE THIS.

M E E T M E A F T E R
C L A S S T O D A Y   No.2

REMOVE TAPE AND PASS NOTE
TO A **BRO**. TELL HIM HOW TO
DECIPHER IT WITH A #2 PENCIL.

SEND CODED MESSAGES

→ **TURN HERE** TO GET STARTED!

GIVE A SECRET BRO-CODER WHEEL TO A BRO.

(IT MATCHES YOUR RING EXACTLY.)

Wheel
1

Cut out
WHEEL 1
along the
dotted line.

Cut out
WHEEL 3
along the
dotted line.

Wheel
3

window

SECRET BRO-CODER

Inner
circle

Cut out
WHEEL 2
along all the
dotted lines —
outer circle,
inner circle,
and window.

Wheel
2

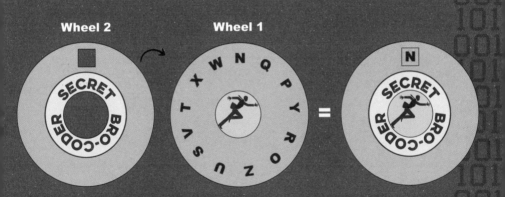

Wheel 2   Wheel 1

Place WHEEL 2 on top of WHEEL 1, with the letter N showing in the window.

Wheels 1 & 2   Tape   Wheel 3

Keep Wheel 2 on top of WHEEL 1. Now attach WHEEL 3 to WHEEL 1 with double stick tape or a piece of folded tape, with the letter A lining up directly under the letter N in the window.

Secret Bro-Coder wheel should look like this.

WHEEL 2 spins around WHEEL 3.

PSST, MAKE SURE N LINES UP WITH A.

SEND CODED
MESSAGES

USE YOUR **SECRET BRO-CODER RING** TO WRITE SECRET MESSAGES. THEN CUT 'EM OUT, FOLD & PASS TO YOUR BRO, DOG, OR SECRET AGENT PARTNER. (JUST MAKE SURE HE HAS THE **SECRET BRO-CODER WHEEL!**)

SOME SLIPS ARE DISGUISED AS RECEIPTS, NOTES & DRAWINGS.

GAMER DUDES DEPOT

ITEM	QTY	PRICE
ANT WARRIORS.....	1	......$39.99
BATS V RATS.....	1	......$42.99
ITEM RETAIL TOTAL...		$82.98
ITEM DISCOUNT/COUPON...		$15.00
SUBTOTAL......		...$67.98
SALES TAX......		...$3.28
AMOUNT DUE......		...$71.26

GAMER DEPOT THANKS
YOU FOR YOUR PURCHASE.

PROJECT
SPIDER
BITE

KEEP ONE
EYE OPEN

OPERATION
SCORPION

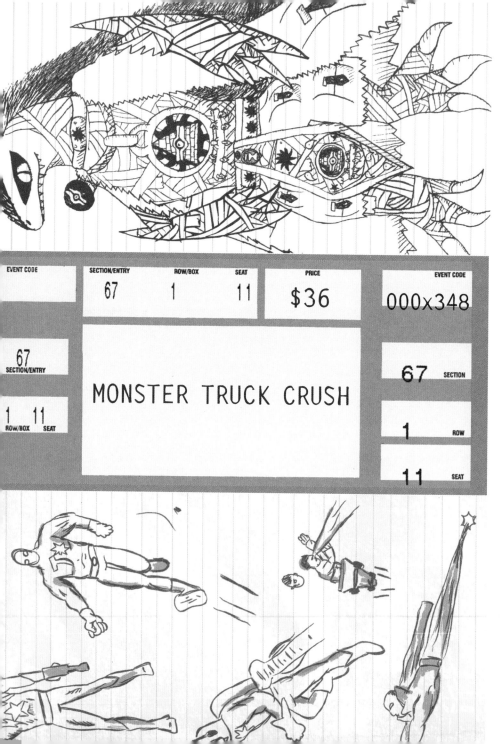

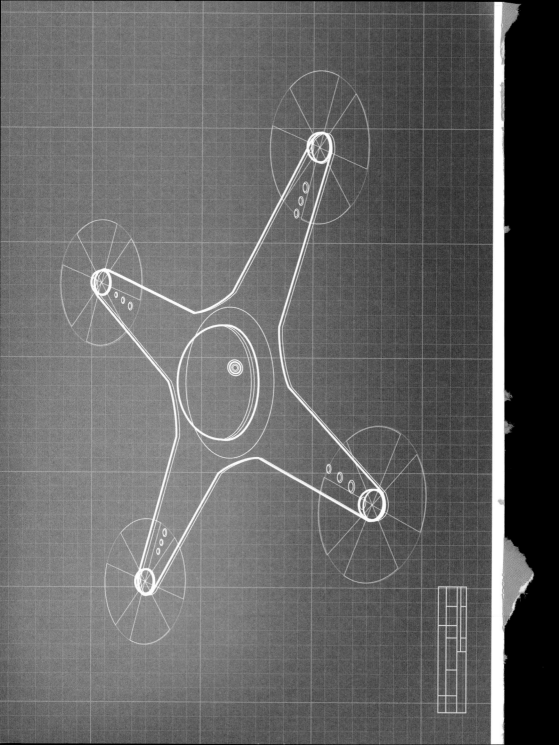

ANSWERS

YOU ARE AN OFFICIAL GOVERNMENT SPY
DOUBLE
SLEEPER
PROVOKER

PROJECT MI AGENT/CASE NO. 135
COVER BLOWN
1. CHANGE NAME
2. GET DISGUISE
3. MOVE

DOT CIPHER
DOG BREATH STINKS

PROJECT PORTAL PRINCE/ CASE NO. 1353
ENTER ANOTHER WORLD BEHIND
A SUIT OF ARMOR

PROJECT KNOCK OC/CASE NO. 8
GOLD IN SUNKEN CITY AT BOTTOM OF OCEAN

SPACE CODE
Double Agent's First Message –
STOP EATING BAKED BEANS
Double Agent's Second Message –
ENEMY CAN SMELL YOUR GAS

PROJECT SUPER SAVE/CASE NO. 86
NOTE #1 – YOU SMELL LIKE A BABOON
NOTE #2 – ACCESS DENIED LEAVE NOW
NOTE #3 – ACCESS GRANTED VAULT OPEN

PROJECT MOLE IN THE HOLE/ CASE NO. 1111
TUESDAY AT
SEVEN PM UNDER
CORNER OF CHASE
AND TRADE

NULL CIPHER
COVER IS BLOWN
HQ's Encrypted Message –
YOUR EARWAX IS OUT OF CONTROL

PROJECT INSECTICYBORG/CASE NO. 006
KILLER BEE
MOSQUITO
GIANT JAPANESE HORNET
TSETSE FLY
5TH INSECT – BULLET ANT

PROJECT GREEN MACHINE/CASE NO. 21
U.F.O. Carving – WE ARE LIVING AMONG YOU NOW
Missing Symbols – ⊐ ⊔ ⌐ ⊏ ⌶
One-word Message – HELP
Deciphered One-word Message –
Enemy aliens coming to capture us take over Earth

ROUTE CIPHER
HQ's Encrypted Message –
SOMETHING IS STUCK IN YOUR TEETH
HQ's Second Encrypted Message –
IT IS BIG AND GREEN

PROJECT MYSTERY MAIL/CASE NO. 48
First Document – THIS MESSAGE IS FROM THE FUTURE
Second Document – TIME TRAVEL IS REAL
Third Document – I KNOW EVERYTHING ABOUT YOUR LIFE
Deciphered Letters – I AM YOU
Who is the mystery man sending the letters? Me

MAKE CONTACT WITH NO. 2
BEWARE OF THE MAN IN BLACK

TIME HAS R